8/02

D1288312

13.95

JET AIRLINERS

FLYING MACHINES

Kelly Baysura

Rourke Publishing LLC
Vero Beach, Florida 32964

About The Author:

Kelly Baysura graduated from Duquesne University in Pittsburgh, PA with a degree in Elementary Education. Kelly has taught grades K, 1, 4, and 5 and was most recently employed in the education field as a reading specialist.

PHOTO CREDITS:
© Archive Photo: page 7; © Comstock: pages 4, 21
© Jay Selman-Avion Photos: All other photos

EDITORIAL SERVICES:
Pamela Schroeder

Library of Congress Cataloging-in-Publication Data

Baysura, Kelly, 1970–
   Jet airliners / Kelly Baysura.
     p. cm. — (Flying machines)
   Includes index
   ISBN 1-58952-005-X
   1. Jet planes—Juvenile literature. [1. Jet planes. 2. Airplanes.] I. Title

TL709 .B27 2001
629.133'349—dc21

00-066527

Printed in the USA

TABLE OF CONTENTS

JET AIRLINERS

Look up in the sky. What do you see? You probably see birds. You may also see clouds. If you look long enough you will also see a jet airliner. Stop and think about where that plane is going and who might be on it. Jet airliners make traveling to faraway places fast and easy.

Looking up at a jet airliner as it passes overhead can be quite a thrill.

5

THE FIRST COMMERCIAL JET AIRLINER

In 1949 de Haviland made the first **commercial** jet airliner. The jet was named the Comet. It could carry 36 passengers. It was not easy to fly in the early days. Most jets back then were made from old warplanes.

Ten years later jet airliners were bigger and could fly farther. Many new companies began building airliners that could carry 100 or more people.

An early Boeing 707-102-B

At first people thought flying was unsafe. They soon changed their minds. People discovered the freedom that flying gave them. They could now see faraway lands easily and quickly. You can now visit people in other countries after flying for just a few hours. The jet airliner has brought the world closer together.

Most countries have airlines that can fly people around the world.

THE JET ENGINE

The **jet engine** is important to **aviation**. Jet engines allow airplanes to travel longer distances. They also make airplanes very fast. The loud sound of a jet engine is familiar to most people. Do you know how it works? Inflate a balloon and then release the air. The air rushing out of the balloon pushes it forward. That's the same way a jet engine works. It takes in air, mixes it with **fuel**, and pushes it out very quickly.

The two jet engines that provide power to the Boeing 737 are located under the wings.

The clover is the symbol for Aer Lingus, Ireland's biggest airline.

The jet airliner's wheels move into a place inside the plane after it takes off. They come back out when the plane is ready to land.

THE BOEING 747

The Boeing 747 is a popular jet airplane. 747s are sometimes called "Jumbo Jets" because they are so big. They weigh about 400 tons (406,000 kg). The Boeing 747 can carry about 550 passengers. It can fly 9,072 miles (14,696 km) without stopping for fuel.

The Boeing 747 must gain speed on a long runway to take off.

THE CONCORDE

The Concorde is the fastest jet airliner. The Concorde can fly 1,260 mph (2,041 km/h)! This is twice the speed of sound. The Concorde was built by the French and British in 1976. It has swept-back wings and a long, pointed nose to help it move fast. When the Concorde flies it makes a loud booming sound as it breaks through the sound barrier.

The long pointed nose of the Concorde tilts downward allowing the pilots to see better.

ALTITUDE

Airliners fly at an **altitude** of 20,000 to 40,000 feet (6,000 to 12,000 m). Altitude is how high the plane flies. The air is thinner at high altitudes. At high altitudes jet engines need less fuel to push the plane forward. This means the airliner can fly for less money.

At high altitudes jet airliners will leave a trail that can be seen for miles.

SPEED

Jet airplane takeoff speeds are about 99 mph (160 km/h). A jet flies between 463 mph (750 km/h) and 599 mph (970 km/h) in the air. One plane is different from all the rest. The Concorde is able to fly faster and higher.

A jet airliner takes off at sunset and climbs to about 30,000 feet (9,000 m).

THE FUTURE OF JET AIRPLANES

NASA (National Aeronautics and Space Administration) is working on special types of airplanes. They will be able to carry many more people. These airplanes will fly much faster—even faster than the Concorde. Imagine getting on an airplane in Los Angeles and landing in Sydney, Australia, only two hours later. You will fly faster than 12,000 mph (19,440 km/h). You will fly so high that you leave the Earth's **atmosphere**. You'll actually travel a few thousand miles through space to get there.

GLOSSARY

altitude (AL teh tood) — height above the Earth's surface

atmosphere (AT mus feer) — air

aviation (ay vee AY shun) — art and science of flying an aircraft

commercial (keh MER shul) — having to do with business

fuel (FYOOL) — a liquid that produces power when burned

jet engine (JET EN jin) — an engine using jet propulsion

INDEX

FURTHER READING

Find out more about jet airliners with these helpful books and information sites:
- www.letsfindout.com/aviation
- www.boeing.com
- www.nasm.edu

Berger, Melvin and Gilda. *How Do Airplanes Fly?* Ideals Children's Books. 1996